Redirecting Science Education

To the memory of my mother and father,
Bessie M. Clark and Frank Clark,
who taught me the value of a strong educational background
and who by example taught me the power of principle;

to my sisters, Mary C. Lewis and Ella C. Richo
(both are retired elementary school teachers),
for their encouragement and support
throughout my professional career;

and to all teachers who believe that all children
are capable of learning and succeeding in school.

Redirecting Science Education

Reform for a Culturally Diverse Classroom

Julia V. Clark

CORWIN PRESS, INC.
A Sage Publications Company
Thousand Oaks, California

For information address:

Corwin Press, Inc.
A Sage Publications Company
2455 Teller Road
Thousand Oaks, California 91320
email: order@corwin.sagepub.com

SAGE Publications Ltd.
6 Bonhill Street
London EC2A 4PU
United Kingdom

SAGE Publications India Pvt. Ltd.
M-32 Market
Greater Kailash I
New Delhi 110 048 India

Printed in the United States of America

Library of Congress Cataloging-in-Publication Data

Clark, Julia V.
    Redirecting science education : reform for a culturally
diverse classroom / Julia V. Clark.
        p.   cm.
    Includes bibliographical references.
    ISBN 0-8039-6275-4 (alk. paper). — ISBN 0-8039-6276-2 (pbk. :
alk. paper)
        1. Science—Study and teaching (Elementary)—United States.
    2. Science—Study and teaching (Secondary)—United States.
    3. Curriculum planning—United States. I. Title.
    Q183.3.A1C55   1996
    507'.1'273—dc20   96-4034

This book is printed on acid-free paper.

96 97 98 99 00 10 9 8 7 6 5 4 3 2 1

Corwin Press Production Editor: S. Marlene Head

Contents

Preface

The quality of education in science and mathematics in schools in the United States is a national problem that has not been addressed effectively. One indication of the severity of the problem is that in both participation and achievement, U.S. students are behind many other countries. Another indication is the low numbers of young people, especially minorities (African Americans, Hispanics, and American Indians), who choose to prepare themselves for careers in science and mathematics. Historically, minorities have been underrepresented in science and science-related fields.

In recent years, the ethnic and cultural diversity of the United States has increased. Changing demographics will markedly affect the composition of the future workforce. The population is changing, and the traditional pool from which the scientific workforce has been drawn is shrinking. Ironically, the greatest growth in the population generally and the scientific workforce specifically by the year 2000 will be by minorities, who currently are underserved by the school system, especially in the area of science. As we progress beyond the year 2000, it is projected that there will be more minority members than nonminority members in the United States. Remaining competitive in a global economy is directly tied to the educational opportunities and training provided to those groups in our population who have been historically underrepresented and underserved. Improving student learning in science and mathematics for all students must be a high priority for the elementary and secondary schools in the United States.

Because science and engineering workers are vital to an advanced industrial society, the enhancement of minority preparation and participation in science becomes not a choice but a national imperative. The United States will fall short of the numbers of scientists and engineers needed and lose its competitive edge if minority students are not brought along. Furthermore, in this technological society, a basic understanding of science is essential not only for those pursuing careers in the field but for all students.

JULIA V. CLARK

Acknowledgments

I have often felt that much of my success thus far and my antici-pated successes can be attributed to a broad educational foun-dation, a plethora of professional and community experiences, important networking opportunities, and a strong commitment to teaching and learning. So many people have contributed so exten-sively to my learning over the years. Unreserved thanks are due to several of my professors. I owe a special debt of gratitude to pro-fessors W.W.E. Blanchett, William D. Morehead, and Kenneth Crooks, who served as my advisers and encouraged me to choose a career in science during my undergraduate years at Fort Valley State College. My interest in scientific research was initiated while studying plant morphology at Atlanta University under Dr. Lafayette Frederick. The research interest was further developed while I was a doctoral student at Rutgers University. To all of my professors, I am most grateful for your guidance, support, inspira-tion, and encouragement. I would also like to extend special thanks to several of my former students who directly or indirectly influenced my thinking on the writing of this book.

I wish to thank several teachers, colleagues, and friends for their encouragement and interest in my professional growth. In particular, I want to thank Dr. William Smith and Robbie Wiley. I thank Mrs. Essie Jones and Mrs. Ruby Jowers for serving as surro-gate mothers after the death of my mother.

Some of my skills were cultivated and the motivation to write a book took place during the years I served as a Kellogg National

Fellow in a Leadership Training Program from 1987 to 1990 and while I was Associate Professor at Texas A&M University. During the Kellogg experience, I conducted a study on women's leadership from an international, interdisciplinary perspective to get a better understanding of what it takes to be a successful leader. The study took me throughout the United States and to several countries around the world to interview successful women leaders to learn how they achieved their stature, and I applied this knowledge to my own goal of becoming a successful administrator. The women I interviewed were inspiring and provided me with invaluable support for my personal growth and development. I am most grateful to all of these women. I benefited immensely from their suggestions. Special thanks go to the W. K. Kellogg Foundation for providing me the opportunity to participate in this unique experience and to Dr. Louis Bransford and Norman Mindrum, who served as my advisers while I was a Kellogg Fellow. They continue to follow my progress in the academic arena. I am most grateful to both of them for their encouragement, guidance, and helpful suggestions.

  The production of a book requires the effort of many; therefore, my sincere thanks go to Alice Foster and the editorial staff of Corwin Press.

  Without family, writing would be intolerable. For individual and collective contribution to this effort, encouragement, and moral support, I wish to acknowledge with special thanks my sisters, Mary C. Lewis and Ella C. Richo, and my niece, Cassandra L. Owens.

About the Author

 **Julia V. Clark** is the Program Director of the Young Scholars Program in the Directorate of Education and Human Resources at the National Science Foundation (NSF). She also has served as Program Director of the Teacher Enhancement Program at NSF and Program Officer at the U.S. Department of Education. She has served as a tenured Associate Professor of Science Education at Texas A&M University; Assistant Professor of Science and Mathematics Education at Howard University; Associate Professor of Biology and Science Education at Clark Atlanta University (formerly Clark College); Assistant Professor of Biology at Morris Brown College and Albany State College; Visiting Professor of Science Education at Memorial University in Newfoundland, Canada; and as an adjunct professor at Atlanta University and the University of Maryland, College Park. She also has taught biology, chemistry, physics, and physical science at the junior and senior high school levels from 1960 to 1968.

She received a B.S. degree in natural science from Fort Valley State College, Fort Valley, Georgia; a master's in science education from the University of Georgia in 1968; and a doctorate degree in science education from Rutgers University in 1980. She has completed additional studies in environmental science at Yale University, in radiation biology at University of California at Berkeley, and in chemistry and biology at Emory University.

Dr. Clark has been active professionally as a member of the National Association of Research in Science Teaching, the American Association for the Advancement of Science, Sigma XI Scientific Research Society, National Science Teachers Association, Phi Beta Delta Honors Society for International Scholars, American Association of University Women, Association of Black Women in Higher Education, and Minority Women in Science, among other organizations. Throughout her career, Dr. Clark has published in both science and education. Her interest in the science education of young children was sparked during the time she was completing research for her doctoral dissertation at Rutgers University titled "Development of Seriation and Its Relation to the Achievement of Inferential Transitivity." Over the years, she has received an award from the Lily Foundation, an Outstanding Young Women of America award, and a Distinguished Alumni Award, and she was a Kellogg National Fellow.

Introduction

The U.S. citizens and decision makers of the future are in school today. When they leave, they will face a world made daily more complex by rapid scientific and technological developments. America is becoming an increasingly technology-oriented society, and to cope with such a world, it is critical that the population be literate in science. A basic understanding of science and mathematics is essential not only for those who pursue careers in scientific and technical fields but for all students—science education can benefit all students. The greatest benefits will only be realized from a science education that includes all racial, ethnic, and cultural groups and science education appropriate to individual needs designed to enable students to (a) develop intellectually and morally and participate fully in a technological society as informed citizens; (b) pursue further studies in science and technology; and (c) enter the world of work. Unfortunately, not all students have access to quality instruction in science and mathematics, and as a result, the number of persons entering these fields is falling behind the technological expansion. Most unfortunate, minority students, those who form the most rapidly growing portion of our school-age population, are the ones that are most left out of science and mathematics. Unless our schools from kindergarten through Grade 12—and even at the undergraduate teacher preparation

AUTHOR'S NOTE: The views expressed in this book are the views of the author and not those of the National Science Foundation.

program level—become more effective in working with minority students or preparing teachers to work with students in a diverse classroom, the present shortage of technologically literate citizens and of scientists and mathematicians will become even more severe. The results will be a society that is not prepared to fulfill the needs of a technically competent workforce or to exercise the full rights and responsibilities of citizenship in a modern democracy.

The writing of this book is a response to the growing concern for the improvement of quality science education for all students. The United States has a mandate to ensure quality education for all students. Recognizing that all students can learn science, it is the responsibility of every school to promote high-quality education programs in science for every student. In fulfilling this responsibility, curricular and instructional methodologies and materials must be reconsidered, teacher preparation must be intensified, and greater expectations in science and mathematics must be made of all students. If the United States is to achieve a position of international leadership in science, our school system must ensure effective science teaching for culturally diverse students through the implementation of education that is multicultural.

This book is designed to improve the quality of science teaching and learning as well as to increase the access of all students to high-quality instruction in science. It is designed specifically for preservice and inservice training of teachers in Grades K-12, science supervisors and science coordinators of school systems, curriculum developers, policymakers, and all who play a role in the education of American students. A major focus is directed toward instruction at the elementary, middle, and junior high school levels. Research has found that certain mental powers must be stimulated at an early stage if they are to develop properly. Early adolescence has been identified as a key period in the education of students in science. Students who find science boring and irrelevant in elementary and middle school tend not to continue in the subject as soon as they are given options, usually in the early high school years.

This book is intended to broaden the impact, accelerate the pace, and increase the effectiveness of improvements in science for all students. The book provides information on the state of science and mathematics in the United States to help the scientific community understand the importance of increasing the participation of minorities in science. It presents brief profiles of various racial, ethnic, and cultural groups to increase awareness and sensitivity to the diverse groups of students that make up today's classroom. It provides instructional methods and strategies for teaching science and ways of adapting these methods and strategies for a culturally diverse classroom. The book contains information on how children learn science from many perspectives that may be culturally related. It also contains a description of the major science education reform initiatives in the United States.

Students need to become aware of and understand the contributions of science to personal, social, technological, and cultural improvement. As teachers make available to students as many models, alternatives, and opportunities as possible from the full spectrum of our cultures, each student becomes aware that every group (cultural and ethnic) exists autonomously as a part of an interrelated and independent societal role.

1

Science Education
for Cultural Inclusion

The State of Science and
Mathematics in the United States

Understanding the Problem

Education in America is facing new challenges. Teachers are called on to provide quality education to all children and prepare them to live and work in a world transformed by rapid growth in new technologies, international competitiveness, economic globalization, and increasing demographic shifts. These challenges catalyzed the United States toward education reform consideration, especially in the area of science.

National reports such as *Workforce 2000: Work and Workers for the Twenty-First Century* (Johnston & Packer, 1987) remind us that the ability of the United States to remain competitive in a global economy is directly tied to the educational opportunities and training provided to those groups who historically have been underrepresented and underserved. Females and minorities, in particular Blacks (African Americans), Hispanics (Latinos), and American Indians (Native Americans), fall into this category.[1] Given the projection that minorities will constitute one third of new entrants into the workforce by the year 2000 and given the current trend in minority preparation for and participation in science and engineering careers, the enhancement of minority preparation in science and technology becomes not a choice but a national imperative. Furthermore, in this increasingly technological society, a basic understanding of science is essential for all students. However, not all students, especially minorities, have access to quality instruction in science. This has resulted in a population that is inadequately prepared to fulfill the needs of a technically competent workforce. As the nation's economic base shifts increasingly toward technology, U.S. students' participation and achievement in science and engineering become increasingly important.

Few Blacks, Hispanics, and American Indians are represented among the population of scientists in the United States. In the years ahead, these underrepresented minorities will constitute a growing population of the pool of American students from which a highly skilled workforce will be drawn. To remain economically competitive, the United States must become effective in attracting, educating, and advancing minority students to the field of science. They are underrepresented at every level from elementary to graduate school. Lack of preparation in science among underrepresented minority groups in the early elementary grades determines enrollment and success in secondary-level school programs and, ultimately, in college and career choices later in life. Leadership in science and engineering in the United States cannot be maintained unless the education pipeline from prekindergarten through graduate school is repaired so it can yield a larger, more diverse group of world-class scientists and engineers at all levels (Task Force on Women, Minorities, and the Handicapped in Science and Technology [hereafter Task Force], 1988).

In the year 2000, it is projected that 85% of new entrants to the workforce in the United States will be females and members of minority groups. With this percentage, the goal should be clear: Both groups should be part of the scientific and technology professions in proportion to their presence in the population as a whole. The United States can meet future potential shortfalls of scientists and engineers only by reaching out and bringing members of these underrepresented groups into science and engineering. America's standing and competitiveness depend on it (Task Force, 1988).

Data from the National Science Foundation (NSF; 1994) indicate that in 1990, racial and ethnic minorities constituted 22% of the civilian labor force but only 14% of the science and engineering labor force. Underrepresented minorities (Blacks, Hispanics, and American Indians) were 19% of the total labor force and 8% of the science and engineering labor force. Asian Americans were well represented in the science and engineering labor force, at 3% of the total labor force and 6% of the science and engineering labor force. Women made up 46% of the labor force in all occupations, but only 22% of the science and engineering labor force.

In 1990, according to NSF (1994), racial and ethnic minorities constituted 20% of the total population. Blacks were 12% of the total population; American Indians, less than 1%; Hispanics, about 9%; and Asian Americans, almost 3%. Women made up 52% of the U.S. population.

Although Blacks demonstrated significant progress during the decade from 1980 to 1990, they continue to be underrepresented in the science and engineering labor force. Hispanics also remain underrepresented, with little progress during the past decade (NSF, 1994). Limited statistics available on American Indians in the labor force suggest that they too are underrepresented in science and engineering.

If the United States is to function effectively in a technological economy, it cannot afford to underuse its workforce so drastically. As a new century approaches, the promise made by America and articulated by Franklin D. Roosevelt over a half century ago must be reclaimed: "We seek to build an America where no one is left out." America must ensure that all children receive a quality education and have access to economic opportunities (Quality Education for Minority Project, 1990). The success of American education in the year 2000 will depend on the extent to which diversity is affirmed and embraced.

Demographic projections add to the need to increase the number of underrepresented minorities in science and engineering fields. Different fertility rates, immigration patterns, and age distributions, and thus death rates, of population subgroups suggest that the 21st-century profile will contrast sharply with that of the 20th century. If the pattern continues, around the year 2030 the total elementary-school-age cohort of the United States could be about equally divided between Whites and all other racial and ethnic groups combined. Over the next 20 years, Blacks, Hispanics, American Indians, and Asian Americans would together outnumber the total White population of elementary school children. The composition of this projected workforce causes great concern in the scientific community and suggests that the United States must make greater efforts in increasing the proportion of minorities choosing careers in science. The role of minorities and women in science will be the key to future national strength in science and technology.

Changing Demographics

In recent years, the cultural and ethnic diversity of the United States population has increased. National reports such as *One-Third of a Nation* (American Council on Education, 1988) and *Workforce 2000* (Johnston & Packer, 1987) document the extent to which America is changing. *One-Third of a Nation* states that by the year 2000, one third of all school children in the United States will be from a different minority group. This situation has already occurred in some regions, such as Texas and California; 37% of Texas's population is made up of minority groups. Within the next few years, the minority-majority distribution in the schools will change, and the number of Blacks, Hispanics, American Indians, and Asian Americans will total more than the number of Anglos (Institute for Education Leadership, 1986).

Three tables are presented to illustrate the dramatic changes taking place in the U.S. population (Hodgkinson, 1992). The tables show the growth rates for various ethnic and racial groups. As can be seen in Table 1.1, different racial and ethnic groups increased at vastly different rates, with the White population showing the least increase. The racial and ethnic makeup of the U.S. population in 1990 is presented in Table 1.2. The nation increased by 22.1 million persons, reaching a total of 248.7 million in 1990. Projections of the U.S. population to the year 2000 and beyond are presented in Table 1.3. Some interesting data can be observed in Table 1.3. Growth in population will take place, but more slowly. America's youth

TABLE 1.1 Percentage Change in U.S. Population by Race and Ethnicity, 1980-1990

	1980-1990 Increase
Total, United States	9.8
White, non-Hispanic	6.0
Black	13.2
Native American, Eskimo, or Aleut	37.9
Asian American or Pacific Islander	107.8
Hispanic (of any race)	53.0

SOURCE: Hodgkinson (1992). Used with permission.

TABLE 1.2 U.S. Population by Race and Ethnicity, 1990

	Number (in thousands)	Percentage of Total Population
Total, United States	248,710	100.0
White, non-Hispanic	187,137	75.2
Black[a]	29,986	12.1
Native American, Eskimo, or Aleut[a]	1,959	0.8
Asian American or Pacific Islander	7,274	2.9
Hispanic (of any race)	22,354	9.0

SOURCE: Hodgkinson (1992). Used with permission.
a. Includes a small number of Hispanics.

population (age 0-17) grows from 64.4 million in 1990 to only 64.9 million in 2010, according to Census Bureau projections (Hodgkinson, 1992). Table 1.3 shows a shift from a decrease in nonminority youths to an increase in minority youths—there will be more minority than nonminority persons in the United States as we progress beyond the year 2000. These data show the importance of minority preparation in science and technology as a national imperative.

TABLE 1.3 Projections of the U.S. Population Age 0-17, 1990-2010

Youths	Number in 1990 (in millions)	Number in 2010 (in millions)	Change
Total youths[a]	64.4	64.9	+0.5
White, non-Hispanic	45.2	41.4	-3.8
Hispanic (of any race)	7.2	9.8	+2.6
Black[b]	10.2	11.4	+1.2
Other races[b]	2.2	2.8	+0.6

Increase in total non-White youths = +4.4 million

Decrease in total White youths = -3.8 million

SOURCE: Hodgkinson (1992). Used with permission.
a. May not add exactly because of rounding.
b. Includes a small number of Hispanics; other races are primarily Asian American and Native American.

Changing demographics will markedly affect the composition of the future workforce, as indicated in Figure 1.1. Of the net new workers entering the labor force by the year 2000, only 15% will be White men, and the rest will be either White women or members of minority groups (Task Force, 1988).

The evidence confirms that minorities are increasing in numbers faster than the rest of the population. It would be in the best interest of our nation to set in motion ways to increase the participation of minorities in science.

What Assessment Says About Students in Science and Mathematics in the United States

In its statement on the conditions of American science and engineering, the National Science Board (NSB) Commission on Precollege Education in Mathematics, Science and Technology (1983) concluded that the nation's scientific and engineering enterprise remains vibrant and productive, although the United States no

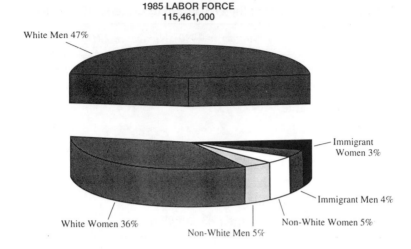

1985 LABOR FORCE
115,461,000

White Men 47%

Immigrant Women 3%

Immigrant Men 4%

White Women 36%

Non-White Men 5%

Non-White Women 5%

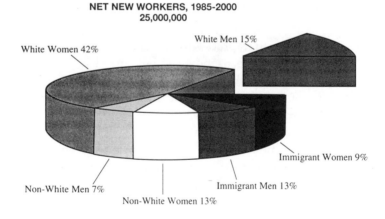

NET NEW WORKERS, 1985-2000
25,000,000

White Women 42%

White Men 15%

Immigrant Women 9%

Non-White Men 7%

Immigrant Men 13%

Non-White Women 13%

Figure 1.1. Changing Labor Force, 1985-2000
SOURCE: Task Force on Women, Minorities, and the Handicapped in Science and Technology (1988).

longer dominates as it once did. On the other hand, the quality of American education in science and mathematics is a national problem that has not been addressed effectively. One indication of the

TABLE 1.4 Science Achievement in Five Countries: Percentage of 13-Year-Olds Scoring at or Above Five Levels,[a] 1988

Country[b]	Level 300	Level 400	Level 500	Level 600	Level 700
Ireland	96	76	37	9	1
Korea	100	93	73	33	2
Spain	99	88	53	12	1
United Kingdom	98	89	59	21	2
United States	96	78	42	12	1

SOURCE: National Education Goals Panel (1991).

a. Examples of what students performing at various levels of the International Assessment of Educational Progress typically know and can do are the following: Level 300—have some knowledge about the environment and animals; Level 400—have basic knowledge of life sciences and physical sciences; Level 500—can design experiments and use scientific equipment; Level 600—can draw conclusions by applying scientific facts and principles; Level 700—can make predictions and interpret experimental data.

b. Students in four Canadian provinces also participated in this assessment, but Canada does not appear because no national score was available.

severity of the problem is that in both participation and achievement, American students in science and mathematics are lagging behind those in previous years and other countries. Another manifestation is the continuing low number of young people, especially minorities, who choose to prepare themselves for careers in mathematics and the sciences. As a result, the U.S. system for education stands at a critical juncture in its history. The NSB called for a new national commitment to provide human, financial, and physical resources commensurate with the importance of science and technology to America's future.

According to the National Education Goals Panel (1991), in 1988 American students scored substantially lower than students in three out of four other countries on an international science assessment given to 13-year-old students (Table 1.4). The United States ranked among the lowest-performing countries in average science achievement on an international assessment that tested

TABLE 1.5 Mathematics Achievement in Five Countries: Percentage of 13-Year-Olds Scoring at or Above Five Levels,[a] 1988

Country[b]	Level 300	Level 400	Level 500	Level 600	Level 700
Ireland	98	86	55	14	< 1
Korea	100	95	78	40	5
Spain	99	91	57	14	1
United Kingdom	98	87	55	18	2
United States	97	78	40	9	1

SOURCE: National Education Goals Panel (1991).

a. Examples of what students performing at various levels of the International Assessment of Educational Progress typically know and can do are the following: Level 300—can add and subtract two-digit numbers and solve simple number sentences; Level 400—can solve one-step problems, locate numbers on a number line, and understand the most basic concepts of logic, percent, and geometry; Level 500—can solve two-step problems, can use information from charts and graphs, can convert fractions, decimals, and percents, and can compute averages; Level 600—can multiply fractions and decimals and demonstrate increased understanding of measurement and geometry concepts; Level 700—can use data from a complex table to solve problems and apply skills to new situations.

b. Students in four Canadian provinces also participated in this assessment, but Canada does not appear because no national score was available.

14-year-old students in 17 countries between 1983 and 1986. In particular, U.S. 14-year-old students performed significantly lower than students in 10 countries, significantly higher than students in 1, and did not perform significantly different from students in 5.

On an international mathematics test in 1988, American 13-year-old students scored lowest among students in five nations (National Education Goals Panel, 1991). This can be seen in Table 1.5. Between 1980 and 1982, students from 12 countries scored significantly higher than American students in one or more areas of mathematics, whereas American students scored significantly higher than students from 5 countries in one or more areas (Figure 1.2).

Test scores on national science achievement tests have shown increases as a result of school reform movements in the early 1980s. Achievement trends for 9-, 13-, and 17-year-old students from 1970

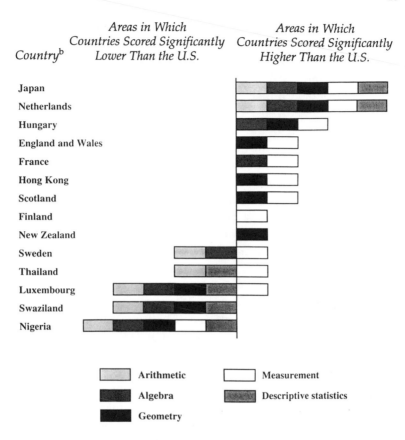

Figure 1.2. International Mathematics Achievement Comparisons: Performance[a] of 13-Year-Olds From 14 Countries in Relation to United States, 1980-1982

SOURCE: National Education Goals Panel (1991).

a. Five mathematics areas were tested. A block to the left of the vertical line means that students from that country scored significantly lower than students from the United States in that area. A block to the right of the vertical line means that students from that country scored significantly higher than students from the United States in that area. If no block is shown, the average score of students from that country was not significantly different from the average score of U.S. students in that area.

b. Students in Israel, Belgium, and Canada also participated in the assessment. Israel does not appear on this table because Israeli students' scores were not significantly different from American students' scores in any of the five areas tested. Belgium and Canada do not appear because national scores were not available.

to 1986 show a pattern of initial declines followed by subsequent upturns for the three age groups. Mathematics achievement showed a similar pattern, with students attaining slightly higher scores on national achievement tests in 1986 than in 1978.

The National Council of Teachers of Mathematics (1989) states that "the image of a society in which a few have a mathematical knowledge needed for the control of economic and scientific development is not consistent with the values of a just democratic system or with its economic needs." The National Science Teachers Association (NSTA) Board of Directors (1991) echoes this as they call for "science for all, regardless of background, future aspirations, or prior interest in science."

Data recorded by the National Center for Education Statistics in 1995 indicate lower achievement of underrepresented minority secondary school students in science and mathematics compared to nonminority and Asian American students. Why is this happening? In a study titled *What National Assessment Says About Science Education for Black Students*, Kahle (1980) indicates that overall, Black students seem to like science but that certain conditions constrict their science experiences. Kahle used data from the 1977 assessment of science by the National Assessment of Educational Progress (NAEP; 1979), which showed that more Black students at age 17 find science seldom or never boring, 27% compared with 17% of White students; find it always or often fun, 30% compared with 26% of White students; and always or often like to go to science classes, 48% compared with 35% of White students. These same Black students, however, report fewer science experiences and find science less useful out of school.

In 1993, the NSF presented data on a 20-year look at science and mathematics education in the United States. The report indicated that in 1992, Black high school students were performing measurably better in science and mathematics than they were 2 decades ago. The report, titled *Indicators of Science and Mathematics Education 1992* (NSF, 1993), consolidates previously fragmented information about the status of science and mathematics in the United States and provides a comprehensive view of where the strengths and weaknesses lie. Some key findings of the report include the following:

- Black elementary and secondary school students have experienced gradual but meaningful increases in mathematics test scores, with 9-year-old students increasing by 18 points (out of 230 total), 13-year-old students by 21 points (out of 270), and 17-year-old students by 19 points (out of 300) from 1973 to 1990. Scores of Hispanic students also improved by slightly smaller margins. Meanwhile, there was little detectable change in the achievement scores among White students, and a gap between White and minority students remained.
- U.S. achievement levels remained about the same from 1965 to 1985 compared to seven other technologically advanced countries.

More recently (September 1995), the NSF reported an update on science education of racial and ethnic minorities (Table 1.6). Data from the report indicate that the number of bachelor's degrees in science and engineering fields awarded to underrepresented minority students showed robust growth in the early 1990s, after a period of slow growth from 1985 to 1990. From 1990 to 1993, the number of baccalaureate recipients with degrees in science and engineering increased by 34% for Black students, 32% for Hispanics, and 43% for American Indians. The percentage increases for underrepresented minority groups were higher than such increases for White recipients (10%) and Asian American recipients (26%). In 1993, there were similar numbers of bachelor's degrees awarded in science and engineering to Black recipients (24,421) and to Asian American recipients (24,504). The number of Hispanic students earning bachelor's degrees in science and engineering fields hit an all-time high of 18,442, as did American Indians, at 1,819.

Although many variables contribute to the differences in achievement level among racial and ethnic groups, the most significant is the opportunity to learn (NSF, 1994). Greater efforts must be made to provide more opportunities for underrepresented minority students to participate in science. The number of underrepresented minorities earning bachelor's degrees in science and engineering is encouraging. The United States must ensure that this increase continues.

TABLE 1.6 Science and Engineering Bachelor's Degrees by
Race/Ethnicity of Recipients: Percentage Change,
1985-1990 and 1990-1993

Race/Ethnicity	1985-1990	1990-1993
White, non-Hispanic	–4	10
Asian American or Pacific Islander	46	26
Total, underrepresented minorities	10	34
Black, non-Hispanic	7	34
Hispanic	16	32
American Indian or Alaskan Native	8	43

SOURCE: National Science Foundation (1995).

Profiles of Our Multicultural Society in Science

Of the four population groups that constitute minorities in the
population, three—Blacks, Hispanics, and American Indians—are
underrepresented in science and engineering. The fourth minority
group—Asian American or Pacific Islander—has representation in
most science and engineering fields that exceeds in proportion in
the population (NSF, 1994).

Black Americans

Although Blacks are underrepresented in science, the number
of Blacks among students earning science and engineering degrees
has grown in recent years. Blacks demonstrated significant progress in representation between 1980 and 1990. According to the
NSF (1994), in that 10-year period, Blacks had a larger increase in
the science and engineering labor force (101%) than in the total
civilian labor force (46%). Black representation in the science and
engineering labor force grew from 3.2% in 1980 to 4.4% in 1990—
considerable progress given that during the same time period,
their representation in the total labor force increased slightly (from
10.0% to 10.4%).

In 1986, Blacks earned 4% of the baccalaureates and 1% of the doctoral degrees in science and engineering. In 1986, only 89 Blacks who are U.S. citizens earned a doctoral degree in science, and 14 earned that degree in engineering. However, in 1991, Blacks constituted 2.1% of the doctoral science and engineering labor force.

Hispanics

The U.S. Hispanic population is the fastest-growing minority group and comprises 9% of our population. It includes Cuban immigrants, Mexican Americans, and Puerto Ricans. In 1986, Hispanics constituted 2% of all employed scientists and engineers and held 2% of all bachelor's degrees and 1% of all doctoral degrees in science and engineering. In 1990, Hispanics constituted 8.1% of the civilian labor force, but only 3.1% of the science and engineering labor force. This reflected an increase of 40% (NSF, 1994) in their representation in both the total labor force (from 5.7% in 1980) and the science and engineering labor force (from 2.2%).

Hispanics remain underrepresented in science and engineering, although their percentage in the science and engineering labor force increased by 40% from 1980 to 1990. This increase is approximately the same as the increase in their percentage in the total civilian labor force.

American Indians

American Indians are by far the smallest of the underrepresented groups in science and engineering fields. This makes obtaining accurate estimates of relevant information very difficult, according to NSF (1994). The limited statistics available indicate that American Indians are underrepresented in science and engineering.

Data from the decennial census indicate that American Indians constituted 0.6% of the U.S. civilian labor force. They made up 0.3% of the science and engineering labor force in 1990, the same percentage as in 1980. In 1986, American Indians were holding 0.3% of all bachelor's degrees and 0.16% of all doctoral degrees in science and engineering. In 1986, 37 doctoral degrees in science and engineering were awarded to American Indians. In 1990, American Indians constituted 0.3%-0.4% of all the broad fields.

Asian Americans

Asian Americans are well represented in the science and engineering labor force, faring about as well as Whites in science and engineering. Asian American scientists and engineers are also overwhelmingly foreign born. According to NSF (1994), there appears to be little difference on the equity measures between Asian American and White doctoral-level scientists and engineers. In 1986, Asian Americans made up only 2% of the U.S. population, but they were a much larger proportion—6%—of the science and engineering workforce. They held 4% of all bachelor's degrees and 7% of the doctoral degrees in science and engineering.

Note

1. Of the racial and ethnic groups that constitute minorities in the population, three groups—Blacks, Hispanics, and American Indians—are underrepresented in science and engineering. The term *underrepresented minorities* is used in this book to signify these groups.

2

Building a Framework for Education Reform

Embracing Diversity:
A Framework for Action

Multicultural Education

Multicultural education is education that values cultural plural-ism. Multicultural education provides a program in which members of diverse ethnic, racial, and cultural groups have an equal chance to achieve academically in school. The program allows all students to view the experiences and contributions of many ethnic and cultural groups as significant to the development of the United States.

Multicultural education affirms that schools should be oriented toward the cultural enrichment of all children. Multicultural education recognizes cultural diversity as a fact of life in American society, and it affirms that this cultural diversity is a valuable resource that should be preserved and extended.

NSTA Position Statement

In July 1991, the National Science Teachers Association (NSTA) Board of Directors adopted the following NSTA position statement on multicultural science education:

Our global society consists of people from many diverse cultural backgrounds. As members of the NSTA, we appreciate the strength and beauty of cultural pluralism. We are aware that our welfare is ultimately dependent upon the productivity and general welfare of all people. Many institutions and organizations in our global, multicultural society play major roles in establishing environments in which unity in diversity flourishes.

NSTA must work with other professional organizations, institutions, and agencies to seek the resources required to ensure effective science teaching for culturally diverse learners if our nation is to achieve a position of international leadership in science education:

- Scientific literacy must be a major goal of science education worldwide and for all children.
- We must believe all children can learn and be successful in science; further, the resources of nations must be committed to this end.
- Nations must cultivate and harvest the minds of all children.
- Schools must provide science education programs that nurture all children academically, physically, and in development of a positive self-concept.
- Culturally diverse children must have access to quality science education experiences that enhance success and provide the knowledge and opportunities required for them to become successful participants in our democratic society.
- Curricular content and instructional strategies selected for use with culturally diverse students must reflect, as well as incorporate, this diversity.
- Science teachers must be knowledgeable about children's learning styles and instructional preferences, which may be culturally related.
- Science teachers have the responsibility to expose culturally diverse children to career opportunities in science, technology, and engineering. (NSTA Board of Directors, 1991)

National Reform Initiatives in Science

Numerous studies indicate that schools in the United States are failing to prepare adequately all students for a world that depends more and more on rapidly changing technology. Many students leave American schools without a basic understanding of science, mathematics, or technology. The students most affected are from underrepresented minority communities. The demand for scientists and engineers is not being met nor are schools preparing future citizens with an adequate background of knowledge necessary to make decisions about their lives.

In an effort to improve the quality of science education in our nation's schools and to make science accessible to all students, several national reform initiatives in science education have been designed. Some of the initiatives have gained wide distribution and are being used in various ways in reform projects at national, state, and local levels. Some are partially being initiated, whereas other initiatives are still being discussed and refined by appointed committees. The most comprehensive initiatives include the following: (a) Scope, Sequence, and Curriculum (SS&C) of Secondary School Science; (b) Project 2061; (c) Goals 2000: Educate America Act; and (d) National Science Education Standards.

Scope, Sequence, and Coordination (SS&C)

The SS&C of Secondary School Science initiative was conceived in 1988. The project SS&C is based on the belief that a diverse classroom improves learning and that students on all ability levels can exchange ideas and learn from each other.

Scope refers to a coherent science curriculum that should span all 6 or 7 years of secondary education and include all students. It reflects the principle that "less is more." The fundamental structure of SS&C places focus on greater depth of understanding and less coverage, with appropriate sequence and consideration for developmental levels of students and their perceptions.

Sequence means that science programs should take into account how students learn in sequencing instruction. Students should encounter concepts, principles, and laws of science at successively higher levels of abstraction over several years. Students need to experience the natural world prior to learning the terms, symbols, and equations that scientists use to explain it. Such sequencing should also use the concept of spaced learning, the notion that repeated experiences in different contexts assist students in building their understanding of concepts.

Coordination refers to building students' awareness of the interdependence of biology, chemistry, earth/space science, and physics in terms of their shared topics and processes and their place in the larger body of human knowledge.

SS&C advocates that instructional strategies be appropriate for heterogeneous groups, with no tracking. Because experiences should precede mastery of terminology, a constructivist approach to learning that responds to students' preconceptions is most appropriate. Student-centered lessons, with emphasis on hands-on activities, are integral to the SS&C approach. The project advocates that science programs should help students to answer questions of science by allowing them to propose and pursue ideas, concepts, and information, not by presenting assertions or authority-determined answers. Teachers using SS&C encourage students to ask: How do we know? What do we believe? What does it mean?

Two documents of the SS&C initiative have been produced: *The Content Core: A Guide for Curriculum Developers* (NSTA, 1992a) and *Relevant Research* (NSTA, 1992b). *The Content Core* was created to guide designers of new curricula. It includes examples on coordinating, sequencing, and spiraling science content as well as a delineation of core science content itself. *Relevant Research* is a collection of research papers and philosophical assertions on how secondary school students learn science best.

Project 2061

Project 2061 was launched in 1985 by the American Association for the Advancement of Science (AAAS) under the direction of F. James Rutherford. Project 2061 is based on the belief that the K-12 education system should be reformed so that all American high school graduates are science literate. This means they are equipped with the knowledge and skills they need to make sense of how the world works, think critically and independently, and lead interesting, responsible, and productive lives in a culture increasingly shaped by science and technology.

Project 2061 is based on six assumptions:

- Reform must be comprehensive; center on all children, all grades, and all subjects; and be long term.
- Curriculum reform should be shaped by our vision of the lasting knowledge and skills that we want students to acquire as they become adults. Included are a common core of learning and opportunities for learning that serve particular needs and interests of individual students.
- The common core of learning science, mathematics, and technology should center on science literacy rather than specifically on preparation for scientific careers. The core curriculum should emphasize connections among the natural and social sciences, mathematics, and technology and between those areas and the arts, humanities, and vocational subjects.
- Schools should teach less and teach it better, not include more superficial coverage of specialized terms and algorithms.
- Reform should promote equity in science, mathematics, and technology education, serving all students equally well.
- In response to variety in state and local circumstances and diversity in student backgrounds and interests, reform should allow more approaches for organizing instruction than are common today.

Project 2061 has produced two major documents. The first is *Science for All Americans: Project 2061* (AAAS, 1989), which presents a vision and goals for science literacy. The second is *Benchmarks for Science Literacy* (AAAS, 1993), which translates the vision and goals of science literacy into expectations for core content by the end of Grades 2, 5, 8, and 12.

Goals 2000: Educate America Act

At an education summit in 1989, then President Bush and the nation's governors, which included current President Clinton, declared that "the time has come, for the first time in U.S. history, to establish clear, national performance goals, goals that will make us internationally competitive" (National Education Goals Panel, 1991). In February 1990, six education goals were adopted by the president and the governors. The goals state that by the year 2000:

- All children in America will start school ready to learn.
- The high school graduation rate will increase to at least 90%.
- All students will leave Grades 4, 8, and 12 having demonstrated competency over challenging subject matter, including English, mathematics, science, foreign languages, civics, and government, and every school in America will ensure that all students learn to use their minds, so they may be prepared for responsible citizenship, further learning, and productive employment in our nation's modern economy.
- U.S. students will be the first in the world in mathematics and science achievement.
- Every adult American will be literate and will possess the knowledge and skills necessary to compete in a global economy and exercise the rights and responsibilities of citizenship.
- Every school in the United States will be free of drugs, violence, and the unauthorized presence of firearms and alcohol and will offer a disciplined environment conducive to learning.

In September 1991, after adoption of the six education goals in 1990, President Bush announced America 2000: An Education Strategy (U.S. Department of Education, 1991)—a comprehensive, long-range plan to move every community in America toward the national education goals. Two additional goals were added to become the foundation for the Goals 2000: Educate America Act passed in March 1994. The additional goals state that by the year 2000:

- The nation's teaching force will have access to programs for the continued improvement of their professional skills and the opportunity to acquire the knowledge and skills needed to instruct and prepare all American students for the next century.
- Every school will promote partnerships that will increase parental involvement and participation in promoting the social, emotional, and academic growth of children.

As part of the America 2000 plan, the National Education Goals Panel was established to measure progress toward these goals, and the National Council on Educational Standards and Testing was established to consider world-class academic standards in the United States.

Two of the stated goals are especially of interest and importance in the scientific community. They are that by the year 2000, (a) American students will leave Grades 4, 8, and 12 having demonstrated competency over challenging subject matter including mathematics and science, and every school in America will ensure that all students learn to use their minds well so they may be prepared for responsible citizenship, further learning, and productive employment in our modern economy; and (b) U.S. students will be the first in the world in science and mathematics achievement.

It is recognized that these two science-related goals are ambitious, as are other goals established at the education summit, and that they will be difficult to achieve considering the current status of science and mathematics in the United States as compared to other countries.

National Science Education Standards

The origins of the development of science education standards for the nation's schools can be traced to the National Council of Teachers of Mathematics' 1989 publication titled *Curriculum and Evaluation Standards for School Mathematics*. In May 1991, the National Research Council (NRC) of the National Academy of Sciences was asked to assume responsibility for the development of science education standards. In November 1994, the NRC published the first draft, *National Science Education Standards*, and in 1996 published the final report.

The project's goal is to create a vision for a scientifically literate person and standards that will allow the vision to be realized. Founded in exemplary practice and contemporary views of learning, science, society, and schooling, the standards will guide the nation's science education system toward its goal of a scientifically literate citizenry in productive and socially responsible ways. The goals for school science that underlie the National Science Education Standards are to educate students to be able to (a) use scientific principles and processes appropriately in making personal decisions; (b) experience the richness and excitement of knowing about and understanding the natural world; (c) increase their economic productivity; and (d) engage intelligently in public discourse and debate about matters of scientific and technological concerns.

The National Science Education Standards are based on seven principles:

- All students, regardless of gender, cultural or ethnic background, physical or learning disabilities, aspirations, or interest and motivation in science, should have the opportunity to attain higher levels of scientific literacy than they do currently.
- All students will learn science in the content standards.
- All students will develop science knowledge as defined in the content standards and an understanding of science that enables them to use their knowledge as it relates to scientific, personal, social, and historical perspectives.
- Learning science is an active process.
- For all students to understand more science, less emphasis must be given to some science content and more resources, such as time, personnel, and materials, must be devoted to science education.
- School science must reflect the intellectual tradition that characterizes the practice of contemporary science.
- Improving science education is part of systemic education reform.

The National Science Education Standards define and delineate standards in six areas:

- Science teaching standards set forth criteria for making judgments about the quality of classroom science teaching.
- Standards for the professional development of teachers of science provide criteria for making judgments about the quality of professional development programs and opportunities for teachers of science.

- Science assessment standards offer criteria for judging the quality of assessment practices employed by teachers as well as state and federal agencies to measure student achievement and the opportunity for students to learn science.
- Science content standards outline what students should know, understand, and be able to do in natural science.
- Science education program standards judge the quality of and conditions for school science programs.
- Science education system standards provide criteria for judging the performance of the components of the science education system responsible for providing schools with the financial and intellectual resources necessary to achieve the vision delineated by the standards in the aforementioned areas.

3

Learning and Cognitive Development: How Children Learn Science

To teach science effectively in the classroom, an understanding of how children develop intellectually and how children learn is essential. The theories of several well-known psychologists have provided much direction and guidance in this respect. Their work has given teachers some direction for establishing and restructuring science curriculum and for directing the learning activities of children, especially those in the elementary and middle school grades.

Piaget's Theory of Cognitive Development

Perhaps no other person has had such a wide-ranging effect on education in general, and science education in particular, than the Swiss psychologist Jean Piaget. The work of Piaget began in the 1920s. For over 50 years, using the clinical approach, Piaget studied the maturation and intellectual development of children. The clinical approach involves working with one or a few children at a time and talking extensively with them. Using careful questioning techniques, Piaget was able to gain valuable insights into the creative nature of children's thinking and how they learn.

According to Piaget, children learn by thinking about what they are doing. He maintains that the kind of thinking each child does is related to the particular level of cognition (knowledge and understanding) the child has reached. The thought process and language development, although related, are actually different systems of development. Piaget has identified four major stages of cognitive development:

- Sensorimotor stage (0-2 years)
- Preoperational stage (2-7 years)
- Concrete operational stage (7-11 years)
- Formal operational stage (11-15 years and above)

As elementary or middle school teachers, it is important to note the following. The stages are sequential, and no person skips a stage. Each child passes through each stage in the same order, but not necessarily at the same rate. The rate at which a particular child passes through these stages will depend on both maturation and environment, that is, the kinds of experiences the individual child has. The ages for the stages are only averages. Many children in the same group may not have developed the characteristics indicated for that stage. For example, the attainment of formal, or abstract, thought—the highest level of development—is not normally achieved by most children by the age of 11. To reach this final stage, children must be provided with opportunities to develop the prerequisite skills of the preceding stages. Because of wide variations in cognitive development, teachers will usually have children in their class who are at several cognitive stages. To teach them as though they were at the same cognitive level would be detrimental to their cognitive development. Teachers need to understand Piaget's four stages of cognitive development so they can recognize cognitive differences in their children and interact with them more appropriately. Some characteristics associated with each stage of development will be discussed briefly.

Sensorimotor Stage

The sensorimotor stage occupies approximately the first 2 years of the child's life. In this stage, at first an object exists for the child only when the child can see or feel it. When an object is hidden from view, the child fails to look for it. To the child, that which is not in the field of vision does not exist. Toward the end of the second year of life, the child develops a sense of permanence. That is, the child comes to understand that objects that are not in the field of view do not vanish, but still exist somewhere even though the child cannot see or touch them.

During the sensorimotor stage, the child embodies those behaviors not mediated by signs or symbols. The behavior is primarily reflective. The child interacts with the environment primarily by using the senses and muscles and is directed by external sensations. Through the senses and motor activities, the child begins to develop behaviors that form the foundation for learning in the next stage.

It is important for teachers to know about the sensorimotor stage even though they do not have children at this stage in the elementary and middle school classroom. It is important that they understand that thought development is a continuous process from birth through adolescence. It begins with action schemes or patterns in responses to sensory stimuli and progresses toward internalization and representation of these actions. This process continues toward fully operational thought.

Preoperational Stage

The second stage refers to the time before which the child performs operations. Piaget defines operations as internalized or mental versions of actions. The internalized actions must be reversible and be grouped with other actions into a structured whole. Operations include logical processes, such as being able to conserve, classify, and combine ideas or objects and place things in order according to certain dimensions, such as height or weight. Preoperational children are not yet capable of logical or rational modes of thinking. Logical thinking skills are for the concrete operational child.

Concrete Operational Stage

The concrete operational stage marks the beginning of operational thought. That is, the child performs logical operations that can be applied to concrete problems. Unlike the preoperational child, the concrete operational child has no trouble solving conservation problems. The concrete thinking child develops the concepts of conservation according to his or her ease of learning: first, numbers of objects, then matter, length, area, weight, and volume, in that order. The child can also make multiple classifications and arrange objects in a long series and place new objects in their proper places in the series. The arrangement of objects in the proper series is called seriation.

A child operating at the concrete stage is capable of *decentration*, which means that the child's thinking is no longer centered on just one property or aspect of an object, but can now center on two or more at one time. The child now understands multiple relationships and can combine parts into a whole. The child develops an ability to reason in a systematic or logical way. Because thinking is concrete and not abstract, the child cannot apply logic to problems that are hypothetical or purely verbal. Only through the attainment of formal thought will the development of abstract and hypothetical thinking appear.

Formal Operational Stage

The development of formal operations is the final stage. Formal operational thought is the summit of cognitive development. In this stage of development, the adolescent child is able to think logically in relation to all classes of problems. The child can solve hypothetical problems and verbal problems and can reason abstractly. These operations evolve out of concrete operations and characterize the reflective intelligence of the adult.

Although Piaget and his colleagues have tried to trace the course of children's mental development, they have not tried to discover how to teach school subjects to children. Their findings, however, have had a profound effect on the development and placement of science content in the curriculum, especially at the presecondary level. Curriculum developers and teachers have tried to arrange and sequence science activities that fit what children are able to do in relation to their mental development level. For example, middle school students are challenged to use their concrete base of experiences to build and develop abstract ideas.

Although formal patterns of thought emerge during the adolescent years, many students do not clearly and consistently manifest this level of thinking. As a matter of fact, most adolescent students do not function at the formal level of thinking. It is important to note that approximately half of the adults in our population do not fully operate at the formal level of development. This is why it is important that more attention and instruction is given at this level. Frequently, instructors have within the same class students at varying mental stages, many in transition from one stage to another. The fact that some adolescent students are capable of, but not performing, formal operations suggests that many of the activities and patterns of thought described in later chapters are appropriate aims of instruction in middle school.

Factors Influencing Passage Through the Stages

A question often asked about Piaget's stages is "What enables an individual to move progressively through the stages?" Piaget (1964) identifies four broad factors that influence this transition and act to influence the course of cognitive development. These factors are (a) maturation, (b) physical experience, (c) social interaction, and (d) equilibration. Piaget views each of these factors and their interaction as necessary conditions for cognitive development, but none of them, alone, is seen as significant to ensure development. Movement within and between stages of development is a function of these factors and their action.

Maturation. Maturation, also referred to as biological maturation, depends on internal factors and refers to neurological development. The development of the central nervous system, brain, motor coordination, and other physical manifestations of growth influence cognitive development. One factor that Piaget repeatedly asserts as affecting cognitive development is maturation, the unfolding of mental "possibilities" related to the physical aspects of the nervous system. According to Piaget, maturation of the nervous system places constraints on cognitive development as well as an opening of possibilities for new development. The nervous system controls potential intellectual possibilities; it is not fully matured until about age 15 or 16. In the classroom, biological maturation is translated in terms of time. Because Piaget has demonstrated that children construct their own meanings and that their intellectual development is very gradual, the teacher's role is to develop an environment that provides them time to reflect on ideas and integrate and coordinate new ideas. Unfortunately, most teachers' dilemma is that natural learning, within the constraints of development, requires more time than today's schools are prepared to give. Piaget places this concern for time in an interesting perspective:

> If you spend one year studying something verbally that requires two years of active study, then you have actually lost a year. If we are willing to lose a bit more time and let the children be active, let them use trial and error on different things, then the time we seem to have lost we may have actually gained. Children may develop a general method that they can use on other subjects. (Hall, 1970)

Physical experience. The child's interaction with the physical environment can increase the rate of the child's development because observation and manipulation of objects aid the emergence of more complex thinking. Piaget indicates that children's manipulation of objects is crucial to their development of logical thinking during the 11 or more years prior to entry into the formal operational stage. The more experience that a child has with physical objects, the more likely that related understanding will have developed. Piaget defends the need for materials in elementary school classrooms by the following statement:

> Manipulation of materials is crucial. In order to think, children in the concrete operational stage need to handle, or else to visualize objects that have been handled and that are easily imagined without any real effort. (Piaget & Duckworth, 1973)

A child must act on the environment for development to proceed. Maturation can open up the possibilities for development of preoperational thought, but without the active engagement of the environment, the possibilities will not proceed.

Social interaction. Social interaction or experience with the social environment provides an opportunity for the child to interchange ideas and interact with others in the environment. Although physical experiences engage the mind in cognitive activity, verbal interaction with peers and teachers provides additional experiences that can promote cognitive growth. Therefore, it is important that the teacher provide opportunities not only for individual work but also for work in groups. Social collaboration in a group leads to an exchange of thoughts and discussion, which inevitably leads children to justify explanations, resolve contradictions, verify facts, or adjust attitudes. Social interaction encourages children to communicate with each other. Piaget states:

> When I say "active," I mean it in two senses. One is acting on material things but the other means doing things in social collaboration, in a group effort. This leads to a critical frame of mind, where children must communicate with each other. This is an essential factor in intellectual development. (Duckworth, 1964)

Both physical and social development depend on external factors.

Equilibration. Piaget considers the fourth factor, equilibration or self-regulation, the fundamental one. Equilibration is an internal self-regulating system that ensures adaption of the individual to the environment through the continual action on objects by the child in the immediate environment. Equilibration orchestrates the companion processes of maturation, physical experiences, and social interaction in advancing the child to higher levels of understanding. This cycle of repeated and expanding interactions between the child and the environment spotlights the child as the mainspring to the child's own intellectual development.

No single factor can account by itself for intellectual development. It is a combination of all of these factors: maturation, physical experience, social interaction, equilibration, and the interactions between and among them that influence this development. If children learn in ways described by Piaget, every classroom should provide an environment that highlights the four factors responsible for transition to higher levels of intellectual development.

Implications of Piaget's Theory for Teaching Science

Piaget's theory on cognitive development has provided insight for elementary and middle school teachers for the teaching of science. Most middle school students are in the early adolescent stage of development, in this book defined as ages 10 to 15. This age range does not correspond specifically to any one stage in Piaget's theory, but it does correspond to ages typically served by many of America's middle schools. The ages from 10 to 15 are important, pivotal years in the science education of adolescents because the ages range from Piaget's concrete operational stage (ages 7 to 11), when physical manipulation of objects plays an important role in thinking, to the formal operational stage (age 11 and up), when students can use rational thinking and abstract thought in the solution of problems. This movement occurs at very different rates for different students. Thus teachers will frequently have within the same classroom students at varying mental stages. Piaget's theory suggests that teaching methods and materials should be consistent with children's level of cognitive functioning.

Here are some practical suggestions for teachers in facilitating thinking and developing rational thought of the students in their elementary and middle school classroom.

Determine the cognitive level of your students. It is suggested that paper-and-pencil tests not be used in trying to identify levels of your students. They can be misleading. A more effective approach is to ask students, individually, to hypothesize about some scientific problem that is not visible to them. If the students fail to do well, it is indicative that they are concrete operational or in a state of transition from one stage to another. Therefore, teaching should rely more on actions using materials and concrete activities and less on verbal instruction. It is important to remember that students in the middle school can be concrete, transitional, or formal.

Use a teaching/learning cycle. One of the important application of Piaget's ideas for educators is the use of a teaching/learning cycle. This involves engaging the student in a variety of exploration activities to bring about disequilibrium within the student. Expose the students to many problems, in a variety of situations. A wide variety of teaching and learning activities is vital. Because many of the students are at the concrete level of thinking, it becomes especially important that emphasis is on the manipulation of objects and materials dealing with concepts to be learned.

If the students are at the formal operational stage, engage them in problems requiring hypothetical-deductive reasoning and other forms of abstract thinking. Require them to analyze procedures and data and suggest ways of improving the experimental design. With the attainment of formal operations, students become able to develop concepts without the aid of direct physical experience. At this level, the activity of the student can be purely representational and independent of any concrete experiences. The student can act on verbally presented conceptual material. Conceptual development can proceed based on the child's actions on written and verbal materials.

Involve the students in group activities. Have the students read or create materials requiring the solving of problems. Try to arrange the groups so that there will be opposing views, requiring an interchange of ideas. Probably, the most important thing we have learned from Piaget's research is that children must be allowed to experience firsthand as many objects and events as possible so that they can develop their own creative powers. Furthermore, students must be able to share their experiences with others, consider others' viewpoints, and evaluate these social interactions thoughtfully. Active interactions (physical and social) of the child with the environment are seen as the most important school-related factor in cognitive development.

Provide opportunities for students to discuss ethical problems. Because the students at the formal stage are capable of determining and synthesizing general properties, theories, values, and ethics, they should be given many opportunities to discuss ethical questions and use reasoning to discover general laws and principles in science.

Above all, allow all students as many opportunities as possible to think and use their reasoning abilities. They may do this by organizing an approach to a task, interacting with other students about a problem, collecting and interpreting data, deciding on a class presentation, or creating something for the class.

In the past, science teachers have largely assumed that the materials they used were aligned with the developmental level of their students. Research findings based on Piaget's theory indicate that this assumption is not accurate. Students vary widely in the cognitive abilities, and at best, curriculum materials and textbooks are designed for an average level of development. In the classroom, the science teacher has the crucial role of mediating, adjusting, and matching the materials to the students. To do this, the science teacher will rely on Piaget's stages of development as they are seen in the actions and thinking of students.

Three Learning Theories

Piaget's theory has strongly influenced elementary and middle school science education in the past decade. However, the research and theories of three well-known developmental and cognitive psychologists in the United States—Robert Gagne, Jerome Bruner, and David Ausubel—have also affected how teachers teach and what they teach in the science classroom. Each of these theories has important implications and offers some different perspectives for the teaching of science.

Behavioral Learning and Science Teaching: Robert Gagne

Gagne is best known for his hierarchy of learning. According to Gagne (1977), there is a hierarchy of learning capabilities, and each learning capability depends on having understood a previously learned one. The student begins with the simplest learning activities and progresses to more difficult problem-solving situations in a step-by-step sequence.

Gagne stresses the importance of developing a task analysis before beginning instruction. This prepares the student for learning something new after the necessary capabilities have been acquired. This procedure forms a foundation for higher-order skills or problem-solving capabilities. To be effective, teachers must take into account what each student already knows and what the student needs to know. Gagne suggests that in developing a task analysis you should ask yourself: "What is it I want my students to do? What do they need to know to do it?" In practice, using Gagne's suggestions, instruction proceeds in this manner: (a) Define the desired product; (b) attempt to define the learning necessary to achieve this goal; (c) define the prerequisite skills to determine the skill-knowledge hierarchy; (d) formulate a behavioral objective for each skill-knowledge cell; (e) construct learning activities; and (f) construct evaluation procedures. Beginning with the simplest and progressing to the most complex, Gagne's theory identifies eight levels of learning:

Level 1: Signal learning. This level involves involuntary actions related to emotions. Examples of signal learning include fright, joy, or pleasure. The responses are undefined and emotional in nature and are not related to a learning hierarchy.

Level 2: Stimulus-response learning. This is voluntary motor learning. The student displays learning in response to a stimulus.

Level 3: Chaining. A succession of stimulus-response behaviors are linked together to form a self-acting sequence.

Level 4: Verbal association. A series of words or sentences whose connections to other meanings are based on previous learning is used.

Level 5: Multiple discrimination. This is acquiring the capacity for making a number of identifying responses to various stimuli.

Level 6: Concept learning. This is acquiring the capacity to make a response to a group of variables.

Level 7: Principle learning. This level involves making a response that includes two or more concepts.

Level 8: Problem solving. Two or more acquired principles are applied.

Gagne emphasizes problem solving as the highest level of learning, with the lower learning levels prerequisite to the highest level.

SOME IMPLICATIONS OF GAGNE'S THEORY

1. Arrange the learning environment so that children will have many opportunities to master various types of learning, moving from the simplest (signal learning) to the most complex (problem solving).
2. Specify the desired behavioral objective, structure lessons in small steps, and present them in a sequence.
3. The lesson must take into account what the learner already knows how to do and what the learner needs to know.

Discovery Learning and
Science Teaching: Jerome Bruner

Bruner is a cognitive psychologist who has made significant contributions on how children learn. Like Piaget, Bruner maintains that each child passes through stages that are age related and biologically determined and that learning will depend primarily on the developmental level that the child has attained. These stages are sequential. Bruner refers to the stages as representations and characterizes them as follows:

Enactive representation (birth-3 years). This stage is mainly sensory. During this stage, the child learns about the environment by interacting with it perceptionally.

Ikonic representation (3-7 years). During this stage, the child develops the ability to form mental pictures of previous experiences.

Symbolic representation (7 years-adulthood). During the symbolic stage, the child develops the ability to use words and symbols for actual experiences.

In passing through these stages, the child progresses from sensory representation to concrete and, finally, to abstract. When children learn science concepts, however, they can learn them only within the framework of whichever stage of intellectual development they are in at the time, according to Bruner. He urges teachers to help children pass progressively through the stages by providing them with challenging experiences.

Bruner's stages correspond somewhat with those of Piaget with one important difference. They differ in the concept of language and the role it plays in intellectual development. Piaget believes that although the thought process and language development are related, they are actually different systems of development. Piaget theorizes that the child's thinking is based on a system of inner logic that evolves as the child organizes and adapts to experience. Bruner maintains that thought arrives from within and is essentially internalized language. The child transfers these experiences into language and uses language in thinking.

According to Bruner, children should learn inductively, that is, from specific to the more general. He set down a very controversial statement about curriculum development when he suggested that "any subject can be taught effectively in some intellectually honest form to any child at any stage of development" (Bruner, 1960).

One of Bruner's major contributions to educational theory is discovery learning. He has been instrumental in leading the movement toward discovery teaching and learning. Bruner thinks that students learn best by discovery. Discovery learning provides children with opportunities to learn on their own through activity and direct experience with science materials. Bruner differs from Gagne in his approach on learning. For Gagne, the key question is "What is it that you want the child to know or to be able to do?" Bruner asks, "How do you want the child to know?" Both consider knowledge as the major objective, but their concepts of knowledge and knowing are quite different. Gagne places emphasis on learning itself, whether it is by discovery, review, or some other approach. Bruner places emphasis on learning by discovery. For Bruner, the method of learning is more important than the product. According to Bruner, allowing the learner to discover information and organize what is encountered is a necessary condition for learning the techniques of problem solving. He maintains that teachers must allow the student to become a problem solver. He suggests that, whenever possible, teaching and learning should be conducted in a manner enabling students to discover concepts for themselves.

Bruner (1961) outlines four major advantages derived from learning by discovery:

1. There is an increase in intellectual potency. Discovery learning helps children learn how to learn. It helps them develop problem-solving skills. They learn how to organize problems and develop strategies in solving them.
2. Emphasis is placed on intrinsic rather than extrinsic rewards. Discovery learning leads to internal self-rewarding satisfaction, self-fulfillment, and self-motivation. It also

improves self-concept and provides the children with a sense of pleasure and excitement after finding the solution to the problem on their own.

3. Students learn the heuristic of discovery. Through problem-solving activities, students learn how to find out things for themselves. Students mastering the methods of discovery learning can apply these same skills and techniques to work through real problems in the environment.

4. Discovery aids in better memory retention. The student is more likely to remember information resulting from discovery. Students often do not recall concepts told to them.

Students learn the discovery process through hands-on interaction with objects in the environment. With a discovery approach, the understanding of science content increases.

Although many benefits can be derived from using the discovery approach in teaching science to elementary and middle school students, it must be noted that discovery learning should not be the only teaching strategy used. Many concepts cannot be learned by discovery, and the teacher will have to use other appropriate strategies to accomplish the learning of these concepts.

SOME IMPLICATIONS OF BRUNER'S THEORY

1. Gear the instruction to the level of the student's cognitive functioning.

2. Use discovery-learning techniques to motivate students, help them to retain information, and teach them how to learn.

3. Ask challenging questions that will get the students to make guesses, or hypotheses, before engaging in science activities.

4. Begin a lesson with a problem, and students will learn the basics as they struggle with the problem.

Expository Teaching: David Ausubel

Ausubel is a cognitive psychologist who favors expository teaching. He differs from most cognitive psychologists in that they favor discovery learning. It is the behaviorist psychologists who favor guided learning or expository teaching and its correlative reception learning. In expository teaching and learning, all the information to be learned is presented to the learner in its final form. According to Ausubel (1963), when the material is organized and presented properly, students can learn very effectively through textbook and lecture methods. Ausubel maintains that the lecture approach can lead to as much understanding and retention as discovery methods.

To assist in the organizing and sequencing of subject matter, Ausubel recommends that teachers use *advance organizers*. An advance organizer is an introduction to content that precedes instruction. It is usually given verbally through lecture.

Ausubel believes that learning should be a deductive process. In other words, students should be presented with a general concept and should proceed to specifics.

Ausubel (1963) believes that students can learn when the subject matter is presented to them in organized and meaningful ways. He indicates that instruction is meaningful when the new knowledge is linked to what the student already knows. If the students memorize the new information without incorporating it into their cognitive structure, rote learning occurs. Whether the new information teachers present is meaningful or rote learning for their students depends on how relevant they make it for them and how well it matches their level of cognitive development.

Ausubel refutes Bruner's statement supporting the advantages of learning by discovery. He attributes the student's organization of knowledge to the structured textbooks and other materials rather than through strictly discovery activities. Ausubel maintains that he is not opposed to the occasional use of discovery learning, particularly with elementary school children in the concrete stage. However, once the students reach the formal level of thinking, they can learn more effectively by reception methods. According to Ausubel, reception learning of concepts is the foundation on which higher learning builds. Without it, he belives there cannot be discovery learning.

1. Use advance organizers either to activate the students' reception system or to equip them with the necessary reception they do not have.
2. Organize lessons according to the process of progressive differentiation, moving from the general to the specific.
3. Learning new knowledge will be meaningful to the degree that the learners can relate it to the ideas that they already know.

Overall, the theories of Piaget, Gagne, Bruner, and Ausubel have provided insight for the teaching of science for teachers, especially at the elementary or middle school levels. They have provided guidance and direction as teachers plan and direct learning activities and experiences for their students. Although each of the theories provides teachers with a unique point of view of learning and child development, most of their ideas are not separate. In fact, the theories of Piaget, Gagne, and Bruner either reinforce or complement each other, and there is much overlapping among these three theories. For example, each of these theories emphasizes hands-on learning and the use of a variety of materials in the teaching of science to elementary and middle school science students. An understanding of these theories is essential in providing appropriate experiences for all students.

Constructivist Learning Theory

In recent years, much attention has been given to teaching science from a constructivist perspective. Constructivist teaching places the student at the center. The idea is that the student constructs knowledge rather than passively absorbs it (Brooks & Brooks, 1993) and that this knowledge is individually constructed by students within a sociocultural context (Lorsbach & Tobin, 1992). Learning occurs within a social context as students share their ideas with their peers in a group setting, commonly referred to as a cooperative learning setting. Knowledge is constructed and modified by individuals within a group context. Learning is not simply the act of an individual learner but a product of social interactions between groups of learners (Barba, 1995).

If appropriately used, teaching from a constructivist perspective can be successful because this approach encourages students to work and interact with each other in constructing knowledge in a cooperative group arrangement. Good group interactive strategies can enhance the cognitive, social, and emotional climate. Constructivist teaching is also congruent with the teaching/learning process of cognitive psychologists.

4

Transforming Teaching and Learning in the Science Classroom

Methods and Strategies for Teaching Science

The methods and strategies of teaching science are the means through which children learn the content (product) and process, thereby achieving the objectives of science.

Teaching an effective lesson involves more than simply presenting materials and waiting for something to happen. A science lesson should be a teacher's attempt to accomplish an objective in a way appropriate to both the children and the material being taught. Teachers are not engaged in teaching either science or children but in teaching science to children. For a lesson to be effective, the teacher must ensure compatibility between the child and the subject matter.

Because each child is unique and all children do not learn in the same way, and because all subject matter cannot be presented effectively in the same way, a variety of teaching methods must be used. No one method of teaching is best for all children, all of the time, under all conditions. The choice of the method should depend on the objective of the lesson, the background of the students, and the area of science to be emphasized, that is, content or process.

There are several methods and strategies of teaching science, including inquiry, discovery, lecture, demonstrations, laboratory experiences (experiments), field trips, discussion, and science projects. Most recently, computers have become popular as effective methods of teaching.

Inquiry

Inquiry involves a series of problem-solving investigations that actively involves the children. It builds on and includes discovery, because through active involvement and reasoning the children must use their discovery capabilities in finding the solution to problems. Inquiry skills develop as children learn how to learn. Inquiry skills involve observations, manipulations, restructuring of events, and interpretation of events. By involving the students in inquiry activities in the classroom, the teacher is encouraging the children to investigate, use prior knowledge in making discoveries, and communicate their new knowledge to others. Both inquiry and discovery teaching help the children develop the art of critical and creative thinking.

Teaching and learning through inquiry takes time. It requires more time than reading about science. However, this time is necessary if children are to discover the answers to problems for themselves. The skills developed during the process and the joy experienced by the children are well worth the time spent in inquiry activities.

To conduct inquiry lessons effectively in the classroom, there must be careful planning on the part of the teacher. The teacher must ask thought-provoking questions that will initiate curiosity among the children. The teacher must reinforce the children's responses.

The ability to use inquiry skills is related to mental maturity. Starting in the middle school and becoming increasingly more sophisticated as students enter high school, materials are designed to stress inquiry. In the early elementary grades, students are only capable of engaging in inquiry activities that require limited cognitive action.

Several benefits can be derived by participating in inquiry activities. Among the benefits of inquiry activities are that they

1. Are child centered
2. Make the student an active participant in the learning process
3. Promote self-confidence in students
4. Develop positive attitudes toward science
5. Promote the development of higher-order cognitive skills
6. Provide for the development of critical and creative thinking
7. Provide the students with many concrete experiences

Discovery

Discovery occurs when learners use their mental processes in assimilating concepts and principles and finding out the answers to problems for themselves. Discovery encourages individuality in children's approaches to problem solving. It validates the fundamental learning style of direct involvement with materials. Discovering the answer for themselves is of prime importance in helping children learn how to learn. Discovery is the culmination of inquiry processes.

Jean Piaget and Jerome Bruner were responsible for a sharply increased interest in learning by discovery in the middle 1960s. Bruner, an eminent psychologist and professor, has been the most articulate spokesman in the United States in the movement toward discovery learning. He advocates that whenever possible, teaching and learning should be conducted in such a manner that children be given the opportunity to discover concepts for themselves. Some advantages of discovery learning, according to Bruner, are the following:

1. The students learn how to learn.
2. Learning becomes self-rewarding, self-motivational, and more easily transferable.
3. It minimizes or avoids rote memory.
4. Learners become more responsible for their own learning.

There are two forms of discovery: free discovery and guided discovery. Free discovery activities are usually for older, more experienced children in upper elementary or middle school grades. In this approach, children identify or originate what they would like to study. In guided discovery, the teacher assumes a more controlling role by helping the child to make "correct" decisions and by supplying pertinent information at appropriate moments.

Guided discovery learning/teaching tries to help students learn to learn. It helps them acquire knowledge that is uniquely their own because they discovered it themselves. Guided discovery is not restricted to finding something entirely new to the world. It is a matter of internally rearranging data so your students can go beyond the data to form concepts new to them. Guided discovery involves finding the meanings, organization, and structure of ideas.

The amount of structure the teachers supply depends on their children's level of development and experience with science. Guided discovery teaching has more structure than free discovery. In guided discovery teaching, the teacher provides the problems, materials, and equipment, but encourages the students to work out the procedures for solving the problems themselves. In less structured discovery activity, the teacher poses the problem and provides the materials or setting; the children have more freedom in solving the problems. The teacher functions mainly as a resources person and gives only enough assistance to keep the children moving toward the solution.

Although many benefits can be derived from using the discovery approach in teaching science, it must be noted that discovery learning should not be the only teaching strategy used. Many concepts cannot be learned by discovery, and the teacher will have to use other appropriate strategies to accomplish the learning concepts.

Lecture

Unlike the child-centered approach to learning as demonstrated by discovery and inquiry teaching, lecturing is primarily teacher centered. In this approach, the teacher dominates. It is often referred to as reception teaching or the textbook method of teaching.

In recent years, it has received more criticism than any teaching strategy, yet it continues to be used extensively. Some of the criticisms are that students usually leave the classroom with factual information only, much of which they do not understand; the approach does not encourage student participation; and many students are not consistently capable of assimilating and internalizing material presented in this manner.

The lecture method is highly verbal, and the information is communicated to the students by the teacher. The teacher directly controls instruction. Although this teaching method is not highly recommended for extensive use in teaching science to elementary and middle school students, there are times when it is appropriate to present information to students in this manner. It can be used

1. To present background information that the students will need to understand or be able to carry out an activity
2. To demonstrate the use of scientific apparatus or to give directions for classroom procedures, such as an experiment or an activity
3. To show students a film, filmstrip, overheads, or charts to illustrate concepts
4. As a presentation by a resource person
5. As a wrap-up to an activity

When lecturing, it is important that the teacher keep it short and present material in a logical way. It is extremely important to monitor closely student attention and understanding during the process of lecturing. The material presented, if it is to be meaningful to the student, must attract the student's attention and interest.

Developing scientifically literate students demands more than explaining content or covering a specified number of topics. Students must be shown how the content relates to the broader aspects of science and society and to their own lives. This is best accomplished through student involvement in laboratory-oriented activities.

Demonstrations

A demonstration is commonly defined as a process of showing something to another person or group. A demonstration can be presented by the teacher, student group, individual student, or a guest. As a science-teaching strategy, a demonstration can be implemented in several ways by the teacher to

1. Show or demonstrate apparatus that the student will use
2. Perform an experiment where there is danger involved, such as toxic materials or open flames
3. Demonstrate the proper use of equipment, such as a thermometer or a microscope
4. Perform a demonstration when there is not enough equipment
5. Illustrate a technique or a concept
6. Establish a discrepant event, thus providing the students an opportunity to participate in group problem-solving activities. A discrepant event is one in which there is an inconsistency between what can reasonably be expected to happen in a given situation and what is depicted as happening. This approach can be very effective for middle school students.

In planning a demonstration, the teacher should do the following:

1. Design the activity so that each student becomes as involved as possible.
2. Go through the demonstration before performing it in class to be certain that it works and that it works in a reasonable amount of time.
3. Outline the questions that will be asked during the demonstration. This is especially important in doing an inquiry-oriented demonstration.
4. Select an appropriate method of evaluation.

When conducting a demonstration, the following points are important to remember. First, make the demonstration as simple as possible. Second, make it easily visible to all the children. Use large apparatus and equipment, such as an overhead projector, if necessary, especially in working with very small things. Third, the students should be continuously questioned during the demonstration. The questions should be skillfully and carefully planned to focus the children's attention on the phenomena under investigation. Fourth, encourage the students to ask questions but adjust the demonstration so that they will end up answering their own questions. Always provide positive reinforcement. Fifth, bring closure to the demonstration by having an individual student or the students collectively summarize what has occurred, and finally, evaluate the lesson—orally or written. In many instances, the summarization can serve as evaluation.

It is extremely important that the teacher displays excitement in giving the demonstration. The demonstrations that have proven to be most successful are those in which student participation is involved. Demonstrations conducted in a mechanical manner by the teacher alone frequently fail to arouse the interest of the students. When students participate actively in giving the demonstration, they become more interested and, consequently, learn more.

Laboratory

The laboratory approach involves investigating and experimenting. This strategy of teaching provides more concrete experiences and manipulative activities than any other strategy. It is a "doing" strategy. Being involved with concrete objects is much more effective in producing gains in achievement than students observing someone performing the experiment, or reading about it. Research has shown that greater concreteness through manipulation of materials leads to greater cognitive achievement. Because of children's innate desire to manipulate things and objects, teaching science through experimenting in the laboratory leads to more interest, excitement, and curiosity than any other approach to teaching. This strategy affords the student an opportunity to discover the essence of science.

Other strategies of teaching science are valuable and should be employed when appropriate, but they are usually most effective when used in conjunction with experiments in which concrete experiences are involved. A student's laboratory experiment is more concrete than a teacher's demonstration, and the teacher demonstration is more concrete than expository teaching. An advantage in involving students in laboratory investigations and experiments is that each student has direct experience with the materials and equipment and conducting investigations. The use of experiments is a valuable means for teaching science, and it should be used as often as possible, especially at the middle school level.

Investigations and experiments in the laboratory are useful to

1. Stimulate interest and excitement
2. Encourage the slow learner
3. Challenge the students, especially gifted students
4. Involve students in problem-solving situations
5. Engage the students in the handling of equipment (activities involving the use of manipulative materials require students to handle and work with equipment and other physical objects)

The following recommendations are suggested for effective science teaching experiences in the laboratory:

1. Keep the laboratory experiment simple and safe. Remember that you are working with elementary and middle school students.
2. The activity should have a specific purpose.
3. Provide thought-provoking experiments—experiences that require students to think.
4. Experiments should be carefully planned, taking into consideration the level of the students involved. Involve the students in some of the planning. As in the demonstration

activities, the teacher should do the experiment in advance before having the students do it in class.

5. Stress both quantitative and qualitative results.
6. Whenever possible, control the variables.
7. Allow time for discussions.
8. Apply the information gained to the children's environment.

In most elementary schools, the regular classroom becomes the laboratory. This can be done as long as there is running water, electricity, and flat surfaces such as tables to work on. The experiments can be conducted individually or cooperatively in small groups. Research has shown that students learn from each other, and valuable information can be gained when they are involved in cooperative investigations.

The laboratory strategy is an important aspect of the inquiry method of attempting to discover answers. The inquiry skills include those skills used to (a) obtain data through scientific investigation, (b) organize the data into a useful form, (c) analyze the data, (d) generalize or synthesize from the data, and (f) make decisions. Inquiry skills enable the scientific investigator to do critical and creative thinking and identify concepts and facts. Facts are the raw material a student uses to understand principles of science. As a student's understanding of science increases, the student's ability to make informed decisions also increases. By using the laboratory strategy, the children can develop proficiency in a large number of process skills while they are discovering science concepts.

Field Trips

A field trip refers to the learning experiences that children have outside the classroom. These experiences are unique and can be an exciting complement to the science program. The following excursions are some examples of field trips: (a) a walk down a nature trail, (b) a trip to a museum or planetarium, (c) a visit to a farm, (d) an investigation carried out on the school grounds, (e) a visit to an industrial or manufacturing plant, (f) a visit to the zoo, (g) a trip to laboratories and research facilities, (h) a visit to places within the school building and several other places of interest. Places to visit during field trips are limitless and too numerous to name—the places listed above are just a few.

Field trips can provide the following educational benefits. They can

1. Enable the children to have firsthand experience with materials and phenomena in their natural environment
2. Provide the children with firsthand experiences with materials that cannot be brought into the classroom
3. Enable the children to observe people working in certain scientific environments. This helps children develop a better understanding of the nature of their work. This can increase the students' interest in science and help them to make certain career decisions.

Although some of the field trips may involve extended and carefully planned trips, many of the trips will take comparatively little time and can be within walking distance of the school. The following are some suggestions for planning and conducting field trips:

1. Whether the trip is long or short, it is imperative that the teacher visit the proposed area at some time earlier than the students.
2. As in other strategies, precise plans must be made and objectives must be constructed.
3. The field trip should have a purpose.
4. The students participating in the field trip should realize exactly what they are expected to accomplish and how they can reach that goal.
5. If a resource person is involved, make certain that the person is acquainted with the objectives.
6. Make adequate transportation arrangements.
7. Obtain parental permission in writing.
8. Discuss behavioral requirements and expectations.

9. Arrange for adult chaperons, such as some of the parents, to go on the trip.
10. On returning to the classroom, help the children evaluate the experience. Have them discuss their observations.

Discussion

Discussion is a method of teaching that promotes an exchange of information and ideas between the teacher and the class. It increases teacher-student communication. It is an excellent technique for review, both in class and in the laboratory. There are several advantages of using the discussion approach if the teacher makes the discussion student centered rather than teacher centered. All too often, what passes for discussion is really a lecture with periodic breaks for students to ask questions. For the discussion to be effective, it must be student centered with students expressing their ideas and opinions.

Some advantages of the discussion approach to teaching are the following:

1. It encourages critical and creative thinking, especially if inquiry questioning is involved.
2. Through their comments, the teacher gets to really know the students and their level of understanding and comprehension. It also alerts the teacher to problems that the students might be experiencing.
3. It increases the students' listening and communication skills.

There are several ways in which a discussion can be conducted in the classroom. It can be an open discussion, which is spontaneous and the topic is determined by the students. This type of discussion is not encouraged for elementary school science students. If a discussion is to take place in the elementary classroom, a planned discussion is recommended. In a planned discussion, the students have an opportunity to express their opinion on a particular topic but the topic has been determined by the teacher. The teacher has carefully planned questions that ensure the participation for all students. The teacher guides the discussion to make certain that it is not dominated by a few students. The discussion can also be in the form of a formal debate. This approach is commonly used when introducing controversial issues. It can prove to be effective in a middle school science classroom on topics related to science, technology, and society (STS).

Some suggestions for teachers planning to use discussion as a method of teaching science are the following:

1. Avoid using the discussion as a form of lecture.
2. Make certain the students have prepared for the discussion through reading, a laboratory activity, or a field trip. In this way, they will have enough accurate information to draw on rather than on opinion only.
3. Give as much positive reinforcement as possible.
4. Facilitate the discussion through planning, questioning, and summarizing.
5. Ask questions that stimulate interest, focus attention, evaluate knowledge, and make students think, both critically and creatively.
6. Give the students enough time to formulate and express their thoughts before answering questions. Research has shown that extended wait time, that is, from 3 to 5 seconds, produces more accurate and longer answers by the students.

Science Projects

A science project is a learning experience in science that provides students with an opportunity to develop knowledge, skills, and understanding on a selected topic. The project emphasizes individual student effort. It involves extensive reading in a specific area, some writing, and an experiment. The success of this science-teaching method is determined by the extent to which the student becomes involved. The teacher role is to (a) guide the student in reading the appropriate information pertaining to the project, (b) provide guidelines for constructing and preparing the project, and (c) provide assistance in locating resources.

A science project can be a special undertaking by individual students or a required assignment for individual students or groups of students. The projects can terminate in a science fair held at the school or in competition with other local school students. Science projects can be constructed at any grade level, but they take place more often in the middle school or at higher grade levels.

Many advantages can be derived from participation in science projects. They

1. Provide individual students with the opportunity to discipline themselves
2. Permit the student to discover a more realistic picture of science
3. Provide students, especially those with special talents, an opportunity to pursue an in-depth study in an area of interest to them

Computers

Computers have become more available to students in Grades K-12. Their use is growing as instructional tools in the science classroom throughout the United States. Computers are great motivators, and the use of them has increased student interest in science and improved science education for many children.

Computers can be used in various ways in the science classroom, depending on the knowledge and interest of the teacher and on the kinds of software and hardware available.

Drill and practice. Through drill-and-practice programs, computers can help students improve their grades in science. Drill-and-practice programs address the individual needs of children by providing immediate and appropriate feedback and positive reinforcement. They also provide students with exercises that review subject matter content. Many of the computer programs written for elementary and middle school students emphasize drill and practice.

Individualizing instruction. With the use of a computer, students can work at their own pace and level of interest and difficulty.

Simulation and modeling. Through graphics and models, situations and experiments can be simulated. Simulations provide opportunities for students to use higher-level thinking skills.

Instructional games. Games contain problems that will challenge the students and increase their problem-solving skills. Games encourage students to participate as role players in realistic problem-solving situations. They are also fun.

Problem solving. Problem-solving programs for the computer go beyond producing responses similar to those found in drill-and-practice, simulation, and tutorial programs. Good problem-solving programs center on real situations that may have significant meaning to students. These learning experiences require considerable student involvement and interaction before solutions are proposed by the students and results are determined and displayed. They present opportunities to develop reasoning and critical-thinking skills.

Tutorial. Through drill and practice, simulations and games, and problem solving, the computer serves as a kind of tutor and can be used for remediation and enrichment.

In the past few years, technology has been rapidly changing the way some teachers teach and the way students learn. Schools are treating and using technology differently than they did a few years ago. Students who formerly went to a computer laboratory for reading practice or individualized mathematics problems are now using multimedia software or using telecommunications networks to conduct global science experiments. Throughout the country, teachers are using technology to restructure their classrooms, implement new instructional techniques, and transform student and teacher roles.

Technology makes it easier for teachers to individualize instruction and for students to engage in self-directed learning. Video, computer, and multimedia technologies can accommodate students with a variety of learning styles more flexibly than conventional materials. Some students, for example, may learn more readily with graphics or sound than through text alone.

An abundant amount of software has been developed for the enhancement of classroom activities and investigations through graphics, words, images, and numbers. Although some software programs are available for precollege science teaching, they do not provide hands-on manipulation with real objects as recommended as important science education experiences. In evaluating the suitability of computer software, teachers should first consider their goals for instruction and then select the appropriate program.

Research has shown that some instructional methods and strategies are more effective than others, especially for science students in Grades K-12. Strategies that are child centered or learner centered tend to be more effective and are highly recommended. These strategies, such as inquiry, discovery, and experiments, place emphasis on the use of hands-on manipulative laboratory activities. Teachers in effective classrooms will use these strategies as often as appropriate. They will devote minimum time to lectures and other teacher-centered approaches.

Effective science teachers will do the following:

1. Provide many manipulative laboratory opportunities for the children
2. Offer a variety of cognitive stimulation and teaching methods to their students
3. Plan lessons in a logical sequence
4. Use the processes of science as basic thinking skills

In selecting the appropriate method to use, it is important that the teacher first know what is to be taught and why it is being taught before deciding how it will be taught.

Pitfalls in Teaching Science

Too often, teachers use lectures as their main instructional method in teaching science to students in Grades K-12. The class becomes very content oriented. Rote learning and memorization are overemphasized in the development of basic concepts. As a result, the students' reasoning abilities are not being challenged.

In addition to the frequent use of traditional lecture consisting of a content-oriented inculcation of facts and the overemphasis of rote learning and memory, there are other pitfalls in the teaching of science:

- Little or no opportunity is provided for the use and development of problem-solving skills. Students do not have the opportunity to arrive at their own conclusions through the inquiry and discovery approaches to teaching.
- Instruction fails to cut across the various science disciplines (and other disciplines) to highlight their interconnections.
- Little flexibility exists in pedagogical method.
- Learning materials are not relevant to students' interest.
- Students are not provided with experiences that will challenge them intellectually.
- Students' progress through various techniques of evaluation are not closely monitored.
- Teaching strategies do not consider a variety of learning styles.
- Drill and memorization are overemphasized.
- Textbooks, audiovisuals, and other materials that do not represent the multicultural realities of the students' environment are used.
- Too few hands-on experiences that facilitate student understanding of abstract science concepts are provided.
- Opportunities for students to engage in problem-solving activities are not provided.
- Cultural diversity is not considered in instructional practices.

Cultural diversity is appreciated in science classrooms because it enhances, rather than detracts from, the richness and effectiveness of science learning. Through multicultural education, teachers use techniques and strategies that facilitate the academic achievement of students from diverse racial and ethnic groups, from all social classes.

Adapting Teaching Methods and Strategies in Science for a Culturally Diverse Classroom

Teaching science in a multicultural or multiethnic classroom does not imply different goals for different groups or individuals living in different parts of the country. It means providing a curriculum that recognizes diversity while emphasizing commonality. It consists of an infusion of information that will allow students to view and respect the experiences and contributions of a wide range of cultural and ethnic groups as significant to the development of the United States.

The methods and strategies described earlier in the book are important in the teaching of science. To teach effectively in a diverse multicultural classroom, when necessary, the teacher should adapt instructional methods and strategies to accommodate the learning styles and needs of the students. The challenge to the science teacher is to explore and develop new ways of teaching science, assist students in understanding and appreciating their personal backgrounds and cultural heritage, and provide opportunities for students to work and relate with members of their own and other cultural groups. More specifically, to be effective in a multicultural science classroom, the teacher should do the following:

- Become familiar with the history and culture of the diverse groups of students in the classroom to integrate multicultural content into the curriculum successfully.
- Provide cooperative learning activities that will provide students opportunities to associate with each other, learn from each other, and gain respect for each other. Cooperative learning is designed to eliminate the negative effects of classroom competition while promoting spirit and increasing heterogeneous and cross-race relationships.
- In providing career exploration activities, use cultural sensitivity in selecting materials, speakers, and role models. Students must see that people of all cultures and ethnic groups have made significant achievements in scientific and technological fields and that a career in science is a realistic option for all people.
- Implement activities that will help eradicate myths and stereotypes of various cultures, especially those pertaining to negative contributions to the development of science.
- Employ a variety of teaching styles and strategies. Make certain that instructional strategies are appropriate for all students.

- Devise activities and exercises that foster success on the part of the student.
- Evaluate curricular materials to ensure that persons from various cultural and ethnic groups are portrayed in scientific and technical careers.
- Above all, create a learning environment conducive to learning.

Science in the K-12 classroom should involve contact with real objects and many experiences with concrete, relevant materials. The teacher should make certain that all materials and media used in the classroom represent a variety of cultures. Teachers are encouraged to make use of community resource people, bulletin boards, and the holidays of other nations and cultures to provide students with a broad international viewpoint. Resource people should include individuals representing different cultures and ethnic groups. This is also encouraged for visual and audiovisual materials such as books, films, slides, and charts. The bulletin boards can include pictorial displays that portray diversity. Field trips should be planned so as to expose students to forms of diversity that they might not otherwise have the opportunity to experience. Overall, the curriculum should recognize the contributions of people of all ethnic and cultural backgrounds.

The students who have difficulty in speaking English or those with a limited foundation in English would benefit from the use of illustrations, pictures, and drawings during verbal presentations. If the materials used in the activities are unfamiliar to the students, the teacher should provide time for them to investigate the materials in an unstructured setting. These students should not fail to learn science because they are unable to read English. If the cultural difference is based in the student's religious persuasion, the teacher should be careful to respect the student's beliefs and refrain from attempting to challenge those beliefs. However, the teacher should not sacrifice scientific integrity and accuracy to avoid topics like the human body and evolution. The same standard should be used to evaluate that student's progress as those for other class members.

One of the primary jobs of the teacher is to help students develop to their maximum potentials by involving them in classroom experiences that will (a) challenge them intellectually and (b) prepare them for a life of continuous learning. Without sufficient instruction, many students, whether they are slow learners, average, gifted, or from other exceptional groups, will show little interest in science. They will eventually "turn off" to science and never realize their full potential in the subject. We do not want this to happen to any student. We want to educate all students, regardless of their backgrounds, and want all students to experience the excitement of science and to know that a career in science is a realistic option.

Although students from various cultural and ethnic groups may differ in physical characteristics and customs, they are like all students in many ways. They have a desire to learn, an ability to tune out classroom situations that do not encourage them to learn, a need for encouragement, and a need for challenge. As teachers work with students from various cultural and ethnic groups, they must use techniques that are flexible and that relate to the learning styles of the students. They must teach in such a way that the students will see the relevance of the material.

Creating Science Learning
Environments for All Students

For effective science teaching in a diverse multicultural classroom, the teacher must create learning environments that are conducive to learning for all students. A positive classroom climate can be created by doing the following:

- Have high expectations in science for all students. Teachers must make it clear that they expect all students to succeed and that careers in science and mathematics are real options in their futures. The expectations teachers have affect student self-esteem, interest, motivation, achievement, and goals. Research has shown that positive expectations increase student achievement.

- Encourage and challenge all students. Students generally have high regard for their teacher. The teacher's opinion can affect a student's achievement. Encouragement and praise can motivate a student to develop and flourish.
- Do not underestimate the capabilities of the students.
- Respect different cultural traditions and mores.
- Involve all students in classroom activities and discussions. Present science as a subject that everyone can learn.
- Obtain and read background information available on students from the various ethnic and cultural groups.
- Make provisions for as much individualization as possible.
- Vary learning style and strategies.
- Modify and adapt materials and teaching to allow the fullest possible participation of all students.
- Make science accessible to all students.
- Incorporate manipulative materials and hands-on activities as regular instructional strategies.

Changing behavior and creating a learning environment that promotes multicultural education takes time and effort. Teaching must be active and intentional behavior. It also requires sensitivity, tact, and a willingness to examine one's own behavior and assumptions. To be effective, multicultural instructional strategies must be continuous and integrated into daily instruction.

5

Shaping the Future:
A Challenge for Change

T he students in today's science classrooms represent many
hues and cultures, with varying backgrounds and experiences.
This class composition is due to changing demographics in the
United States, especially among the young. As American society
changes, so must American education. Teachers must respond flexibly and resourcefully to change in the student population. Teachers must explore and develop new ways of teaching science to
meet the needs and interests of all the students. The development
of students' skills and capabilities to learn continuously and effectively to develop to their full potential should be a goal of all teachers. Raising science and mathematics achievement of all groups is
important in meeting the challenges of the next century. As reported by the Education Commission of the States (1990) in *The
Education Agenda 1990,* to serve the needs and aspiration of all
Americans, and to fulfill the promise of American democracy, our
education system must display and encourage inclusiveness for all
racial, ethnic, and cultural groups. It must promote the development of curricula that reflect a multicultural society.

It is well documented that minority students are underrepresented and underserved in science and mathematics. At a time
when their numbers are growing, minority students are underrepresented among students doing well in science and mathematics
and among those who go on to pursue careers in these fields. Stu-

dents need to be encouraged and given the adequate preparation to enter careers in science and science-related fields. It is for the collective benefit of society that the numbers of minority group students taking science and mathematics courses at the precollege level and earning degrees in these fields in college be increased. If the situation is not corrected, the United States will suffer immensely—it will be robbed of potential producers of new technology and citizens capable of functioning in their world. Increased minority participation in science and mathematics is an important goal to be realized for the social, economic, intellectual, and cultural well-being of all persons. To fail to develop and use talents of certain segments of our population is to neglect a vital resource, a mistake that we can ill afford to make.

An unfortunate reality that characterizes the problem of many minority students in science education is that the burden of understaffed and underequipped schools usually falls on minority communities. This phenomenon can be especially harmful to a science curriculum because well-trained teachers and laboratory experiences are essential. Inequities in school funding can highlight the social context of schooling. Even in many situations where adequate staffing and laboratory facilities are available, the content and pedagogy provided in science are not appropriate to meet the needs of the diversity of students in the classroom. Children learn in different ways. Staff development programs should be provided for teachers to learn how to change their teaching methodology and styles to meet varied learning modalities of their students. Teachers need to become familiar with the various students' cultural backgrounds, values, and cognitive learning styles that they bring to the classroom.

To ensure that all students receive an appropriate, high-quality science education, measures should be taken by educators to ensure that underrepresented minorities have improved opportunities and greater encouragement to participate fully in science and mathematics education. Curricular and instructional methodologies need to be reconsidered. Curriculum reform and innovative teaching methods should include cooperative learning and alternative learning styles. Teachers should include work representative of various cultures in their instruction. The science program should be designed to foster enthusiasm, interest, and competence both for pursuing careers in the field and for the acquisition of skills and knowledge demanded by an increasingly technological society and workplace.

Science education must be redirected to cultivating the scientific talents of all students, especially underrepresented minorities. This redirection is linked to the historical underrepresentation of these students in the fields of science. America is becoming aware that future shortfalls of scientists and engineers can only be met by bringing minorities into the pool of science and mathematics majors. Responsiveness to change—to differences in students, new teaching styles, new and urgent needs—is essential for effective teaching in the 21st century. The success of American education in the 21st century will depend on the extent to which we affirm and embrace diversity.

References and Suggested Readings

References

American Association for the Advancement of Science. (1989). *Science for all Americans: Project 2061*. Washington, DC: Author.

American Association for the Advancement of Science. (1993). *Benchmarks for science literacy*. Washington, DC: Author.

American Council on Education. (1988). *One-third of a nation* (Report by the Commission on Minority Participation in Education and American Life). Washington, DC: Author.

Ausubel, D. (1963). *Educational psychology: A cognitive viewpoint*. New York: Holt, Rinehart & Winston.

Barba, R. H. (1995). *Science in the multicultural classroom*. Boston: Allyn & Bacon.

Brooks, J. G., & Brooks, M. G. (1993). *In search of understanding the case for constructivist classrooms*. Alexandria, VA: Association for Supervision and Curriculum Development.

Bruner, J. (1960). *The process of education*. Cambridge, MA: Harvard University Press.

Bruner, J. (1961). The act of discovery. *Harvard Educational Review, 31*, 21-32.

Duckworth, E. (1964). Piaget rediscovered. In R. E. Ripple & V. N. Rockcastle (Eds.), *Piaget rediscovered*. Ithaca, NY: Cornell University Press.

Education Commission of the States. (1990). *The education agenda 1990.* Denver, CO: Author.

Gagne, R. (1977). *The conditions of learning.* New York: Holt, Rinehart & Winston.

Hall, E. (1970, May). A conversation with Jean Piaget and Barbel Inhelder. *Psychology Today,* pp. 225-252.

Hodgkinson, H. L. (1992). *A demographic look at tomorrow.* Washington, DC: Institute for Education Leadership, Center for Demographic Policy.

Institute for Education Leadership. (1986). Texas: The state and the educational system. In *Institute of Texas Elementary Principals and Supervisors Association Newsletter.* Washington, DC: Author.

Johnston, W. B., & Packer, A. E. (1987). *Workforce 2000: Work and Workers for the Twenty-First Century.* Indianapolis, IN: Hudson Institute.

Kahle, J. B. (1980). *What national assessment says about science education for Black students.* Bloomington, IN: Phi Delta Kappan.

Lorsbach, A., & Tobin, K. (1992). Constructivism as a referent for science teaching. *National Association for Research in Science Teaching, 30.*

National Assessment of Educational Progress. (1979). *A summary of results from the 1976-77 national assessment of science.* Denver, CO: Education Commission of the States.

National Center for Education Statistics. (1995). *Understanding racial-ethnic differences in secondary school science and mathematics achievement* (Research and development report). Washington, DC: U.S. Department of Education.

National Council of Teachers of Mathematics. (1989). *Curriculum and evaluation standards for school mathematics.* Washington, DC: Author.

National Education Goals Panel. (1991). *The national education goals report: Building a nation of learners.* Washington, DC: U.S. Government Printing Office.

National Research Council. (1994, November). *National science education standards* (Draft). Washington, DC: National Academy of Sciences.

National Research Council. (1996). *National science education standards.* Washington, DC: National Academy of Sciences.

National Science Board Commission on Precollege Education in Mathematics, Science and Technology. (1983). *Educating Americans for the 21st century.* Washington, DC: National Science Foundation.

National Science Foundation. (1993). *Indicators of science and mathematics education: 1992.* Washington, DC: Author.

National Science Foundation. (1994). *Women, minorities, and persons with disabilities in science and engineering.* Washington, DC: Author.

National Science Foundation. (1995, September). *More S&E bachelor's degrees are being earned by racial/ethnic minorities* (Data brief, Division of Science Resources Studies, No. 12). Arlington, VA: Author.

National Science Teachers Association. (1992a). *Scope, sequence, and coordination of secondary school science: Vol. 1. The content core: A guide for curriculum developers.* Washington, DC: Author.

National Science Teachers Association. (1992b). *Scope, sequence, and coordination of secondary school science: Vol. 2. Relevant research.* Washington, DC: Author.

National Science Teachers Association Board of Directors. (1991, July). *An NSTA position statement: Multicultural science education.* Arlington, VA: National Science Teachers Association.

Piaget, J. (1964). Development and learning. In R. E. Ripple & V. N. Rockcastle (Eds.), *Piaget rediscovered.* Ithaca, NY: Cornell University Press.

Piaget, J., & Duckworth, E. (1973, October). Piaget takes a teacher's look. *Learning,* pp. 22-27.

Quality Education for Minority (QEM) Project. (1990). *Education that works: An action plan for the education of minorities.* Cambridge: MIT, QEM Project.

Task Force on Women, Minorities, and the Handicapped in Science and Technology. (1988, September). *Changing America: The new face of science and engineering* (Interim report). Washington, DC: Author. (Available from Task Force on Women, Minorities, and the Handicapped in Science and Technology, 330 C Street SW, Washington, DC 20201)

U.S. Department of Education. (1991). *America 2000: An education strategy.* Washington, DC: U.S. Government Printing Office.

Suggested Readings

Allen-Sommerville, L. (1994). Middle level science in a multicultural society. *Science Scope, 17*(6).

Berryman, S. (1983). *Who will do science?* New York: Rockefeller Foundation.

Clark, J. V. (1979, April). Science delights students. *Atlanta Journal and Constitution.*

Clark, J. V. (1985). The status of science and mathematics in historically Black colleges and universities. *Science Education, 69,* 673-679.

Clark, J. V. (1985, July). Needed—More Black math and science teachers. *Houston Chronicle.*

Clark, J. V. (1986). The science education of women in American and Canadian schools. *Journal of Human Behavior and Learning, 3*(2).

Clark, J. V. (1986, May). Why Blacks shun science. *Dallas News.*

Clark, J. V. (1987). A critical examination of factors contributing to minority participation in science. *Explorations in Ethnic Studies, 10*(2).

Clark, J. V. (1993). Black women in science: Implications for improved participation. In *Science for all cultures* (pp. 20-24). Arlington, VA: National Science Teachers Association.

Esler, W. K., & Esler, M. K. (1993). *Teaching elementary science.* Belmont, CA: Wadsworth.

Hampton, E., & Gallegos, C. (1994). Science for all students. *Science Scope, 17*(6).

National Center for Education Statistics. (1992). *Condition of education.* Washington, DC: U.S. Department of Education.

National Center for Education Statistics. (1992). *The 1990 science report card: NAEP's assessment of fourth, eighth, and twelfth graders.* Washington, DC: U.S. Department of Education.

National Commission on Excellence in Education. (1983). *A nation at risk: The imperative for educational reform.* Washington, DC: U.S. Department of Education.

National Research Council. (1989). *Everybody counts: A report to the nation on the future of mathematics education.* Washington, DC: National Academy Press.

National Science Foundation. (1993). *New report offers 20-year look at math and science education in U.S.* (News report). Washington, DC: National Science Foundation, Office of Legislative and Public Affairs.

Oakes, J. (1990). *Lost talent: The underparticipation of women, minorities, and disabled persons in science.* Santa Monica, CA: RAND.

Office of Civil Rights. (1992). *What schools can do to improve math and science achievement by minority and female students.* Washington, DC: U.S. Department of Education.

Rowe, M. B. (1977). The forum: Why don't Blacks pick science? *Science Teacher, 44,* 34-35.

Victor, E. (1985). *Science for the elementary school.* New York: Macmillan.

CORWIN
PRESS

The Corwin Press logo—a raven striding across an open book—represents the happy union of courage and learning. We are a professional-level publisher of books and journals for K–12 educators, and we are committed to creating and providing resources that embody these qualities. Corwin's motto is "Success for All Learners."